The aims and purpose of this book by Bingo Aki

ABOUT THE AUTHOR

Bingo Aki is an artist. He was born in Hiroshima, Japan, in 1948. He graduated from Tokyo National University of Fine Arts and Music where he studied Japanese painting. After he graduated, Mr. Aki's works were displayed in solo exhibitions all over Japan. He also has a passion for picture books. He was awarded the Japan Picture Book Prize in 2009. Today, he partners with educational experts and creates all kinds of educational materials.

Creativity is the power to make something new. Our children can't be expected to develop a creative mind solely by attending school. Creativity is something that needs to be encouraged at home as well—and the earlier, the better.

Imagine academic ability is like a car. It will take children to places they need to go to in life. Creative ability, however, is like a jet airplane. Creativity will propel children into a whole different stratosphere. It will allow them to become as free as birds flying in the sky.

So, how do we develop creativity? And how does it combine with work? In my case, it's by simply doing and learning from my mistakes. I take action without waiting for inspiration. To begin, I prepare my pencil and paper and launch on a writing spree. I don't think; I just let my hands go. I work without resting. It seems that the brain spontaneously makes discoveries simply by thinking about a certain thing for a while. The brain seeks and ideas come. That is inspiration—the discovery of something new.

In order to develop creativity, concentration is just as important as inspiration. To use our earlier analogy, a jet airplane can zoom thousands of miles above the earth, but first it must gain enough speed to lift off from the runway.

One of the world's greatest inventors, Thomas Edison, said, "Genius is 1 percent inspiration and 99 percent perspiration." The same can be said for creativity.

I created these books to help children develop concentration skills and cognitive ability. All your child needs to take advantage of these books is a pencil. In doing these exercises, children will improve their concentration, and train their brains to seek and discover.

While using these books, children should try to improve their skills by decreasing the amount of time it takes to do the exercises. They will need to do the exercises over and over again, and strive to eliminate errors and mental blocks.

These books represent my inspiration and creativity. I believe that by using them, your child will likewise develop his or her own powers of concentration, cognitive ability, inspiration and, finally, creativity.

Records

To parents

- Time how long it takes for your child to finish each page and fill in your child's log below.
- Please compare your child's record at the beginning of the workbook to his or her time at the end. You might notice your child is becoming faster at finishing his or her work.
- When your child has finished each page, please offer lots of praise.

1 animals (matching 4)	**17** produce (matching 8)	**33** animals (matching 14)	**49** insects (matching 18)
2 animals (matching 4)	**18** flowers (matching 8)	**34** fish (matching 14)	**50** birds (matching 18)
3 animals (matching 4)	**19** insects (matching 8)	**35** produce (matching 14)	**51** animals (matching 20)
4 fish (matching 4)	**20** birds (matching 8)	**36** flowers (matching 14)	**52** fish (matching 20)
5 produce (matching 4)	**21** animals (matching 10)	**37** insects (matching 14)	**53** produce (matching 20)
6 flowers (matching 4)	**22** fish (matching 10)	**38** birds (matching 14)	**54** flowers (matching 20)
7 insects (matching 4)	**23** produce (matching 10)	**39** animals (matching 16)	**55** insects (matching 20)
8 birds (matching 4)	**24** flowers (matching 10)	**40** fish (matching 16)	**56** birds (matching 20)
9 animals (matching 6)	**25** insects (matching 10)	**41** produce (matching 16)	**57** objects (matching 20)
10 fish (matching 6)	**26** birds (matching 10)	**42** flowers (matching 16)	**58** objects (matching 20)
11 produce (matching 6)	**27** animals (matching 12)	**43** insects (matching 16)	**59** objects (matching 20)
12 flowers (matching 6)	**28** fish (matching 12)	**44** birds (matching 16)	**60** objects (matching 20)
13 insects (matching 6)	**29** produce (matching 12)	**45** animals (matching 18)	**61** objects (matching 20)
14 birds (matching 6)	**30** flowers (matching 12)	**46** fish (matching 18)	**62** objects (matching 20)
15 animals (matching 8)	**31** insects (matching 12)	**47** produce (matching 18)	
16 fish (matching 8)	**32** birds (matching 12)	**48** flowers (matching 18)	

Great job! You completed the book!

Circle the matching animals.

giraffe

squirrel

elephant

panda

panda

elephant

giraffe

squirrel

■ Circle the matching animals.

DATE   NAME   TIME

giraffe

elephant

squirrel

panda

panda

giraffe

elephant

squirrel

Circle the matching animals.

Perfect within 10 seconds		**Great** within 30 seconds		**Fair** within 1 minute	
Excellent within 15 seconds		**Very good** within 40 seconds		**Satisfactory** within 2 minutes	
Super within 20 seconds		**Good** within 50 seconds		**Keep Trying** more than 2 minutes	

DATE   NAME   TIME

squirrel

panda

giraffe

elephant

elephant

panda

squirrel

giraffe

🚀 **Perfect** within 10 seconds	🚌 **Great** within 30 seconds	🚲 **Fair** within 1 minute
✈️ **Excellent** within 15 seconds	🚗 **Very good** within 40 seconds	🛴 **Satisfactory** within 2 minutes
🚁 **Super** within 20 seconds	🐴 **Good** within 50 seconds	🏃 **Keep Trying** more than 2 minutes

DATE   NAME   TIME

salmon

ray

eel

tuna

eel

tuna

salmon

ray

5 At the Farmer's Market (Matching 4)

	Perfect within 10 seconds		Great within 30 seconds		Fair within 1 minute
	Excellent within 15 seconds		Very good within 40 seconds		Satisfactory within 2 minutes
	Super within 20 seconds		Good within 50 seconds		Keep Trying more than 2 minutes

■ Circle the matching produce.

DATE   NAME   TIME

strawberry

tomato

cucumber

cucumber

green pepper

green pepper

tomato

strawberry

Picking Flowers

(Matching 4)

■ Circle the matching flowers.

DATE   NAME   TIME

sunflower

rose

lily of the valley

violet

violet

lily of the valley

rose

sunflower

Circle the matching insects.

DATE   NAME   TIME

bee

ant

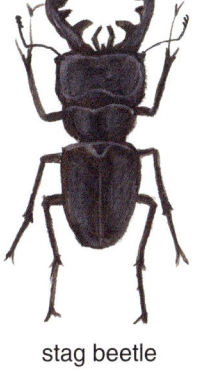

stag beetle

grasshopper

grasshopper

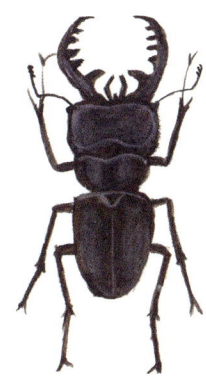

stag beetle

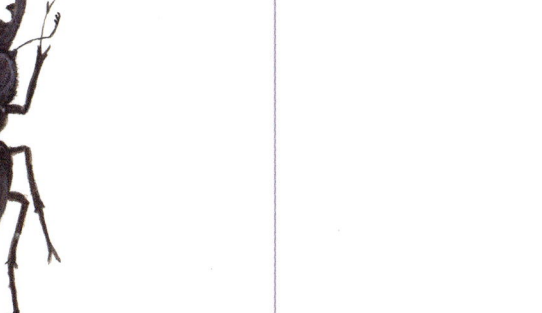

bee

ant

Birds of a Feather Stay Together (Matching 4)

■ Circle the matching birds.

🚀 **Perfect** within 10 seconds	🚌 **Great** within 30 seconds	🚲 **Fair** within 1 minute
✈️ **Excellent** within 15 seconds	🚗 **Very good** within 40 seconds	🧍 **Satisfactory** within 2 minutes
🚁 **Super** within 20 seconds	🐎 **Good** within 50 seconds	🏃 **Keep Trying** more than 2 minutes

DATE   NAME   TIME

duck

canary

parrot

chicken

parrot

canary

chicken

duck

Exploring the Zoo
(Matching 6)

Circle the matching animals.

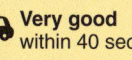

	Perfect within 10 seconds		Great within 30 seconds		Fair within 1 minute
Excellent within 15 seconds		Very good within 40 seconds		Satisfactory within 2 minutes
Super within 20 seconds		Good within 50 seconds		Keep Trying more than 2 minutes

DATE   NAME   TIME

elephant

crocodile

squirrel

panda

giraffe

tortoise

panda

giraffe

squirrel

crocodile

elephant

tortoise

■ Circle the matching fish.

DATE   NAME   TIME

tuna

carp

loach

eel

ray

salmon

carp

ray

eel

salmon

tuna

loach

■ Circle the matching produce.

DATE   NAME   TIME

grape

tomato

cucumber

strawberry

green pepper

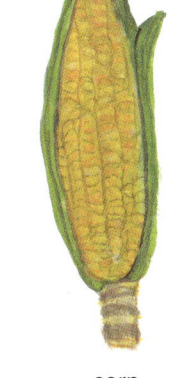

corn

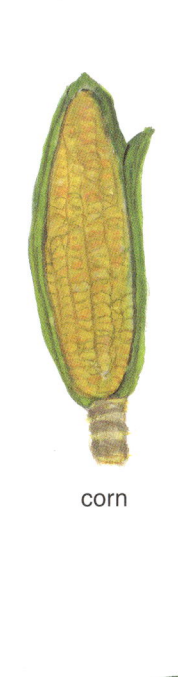

corn

green pepper

strawberry

cucumber

grape

tomato

■ Circle the matching flowers.

| DATE | NAME | TIME |

dandelion

cactus

rose

lily of the valley

violet

sunflower

sunflower

dandelion

cactus

rose

lily of the valley

violet

Catch the Bug

(Matching 6)

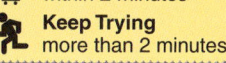

Perfect within 10 seconds	**Great** within 30 seconds	**Fair** within 1 minute
Excellent within 15 seconds	**Very good** within 40 seconds	**Satisfactory** within 2 minutes
Super within 20 seconds	**Good** within 50 seconds	**Keep Trying** more than 2 minutes

■ Circle the matching insects.

DATE   NAME   TIME

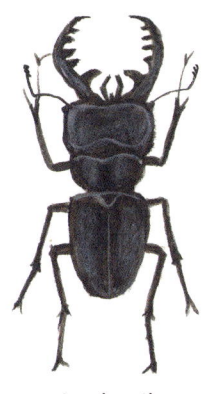

stag beetle

ant

cricket

grasshopper

cicada

bee

cicada

grasshopper

cricket

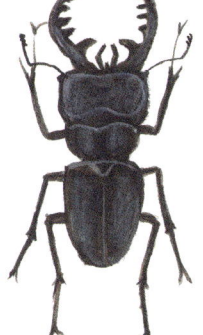

stag beetle

ant

bee

Birds of a Feather Stay Together (Matching 6)

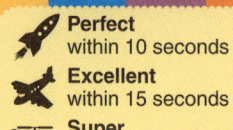 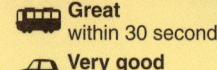

Perfect within 10 seconds	**Great** within 30 seconds	**Fair** within 1 minute
Excellent within 15 seconds	**Very good** within 40 seconds	**Satisfactory** within 2 minutes
Super within 20 seconds	**Good** within 50 seconds	**Keep Trying** more than 2 minutes

DATE   NAME   TIME

■ Circle the matching birds.

duck

peacock

crow

canary

parrot

chicken

parrot

chicken

duck

crow

peacock

canary

■ Circle the matching animals.

DATE   NAME   TIME

mole

tortoise

panda

elephant

giraffe

guinea pig

elephant

squirrel

mole

tortoise

crocodile

squirrel

giraffe

crocodile

panda

guinea pig

■ Circle the matching fish.

DATE   NAME   TIME

tuna

carp

anchovy

ray

carp

ray

loach

salmon

eel

blowfish

anchovy

eel

loach

salmon

tuna

blowfish

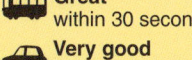 **Perfect** within 10 seconds	**Great** within 30 seconds	**Fair** within 1 minute
Excellent within 15 seconds	**Very good** within 40 seconds	**Satisfactory** within 2 minutes
Super within 20 seconds	**Good** within 50 seconds	**Keep Trying** more than 2 minutes

Circle the matching produce.

DATE   NAME   TIME

tomato

strawberry

cabbage

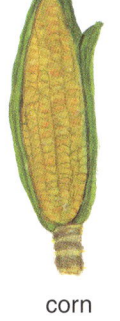

corn

banana

green pepper

grape

banana

cucumber

cucumber

green pepper

tomato

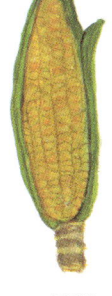

corn

cabbage

strawberry

grape

■ Circle the matching flowers.

DATE   NAME   TIME

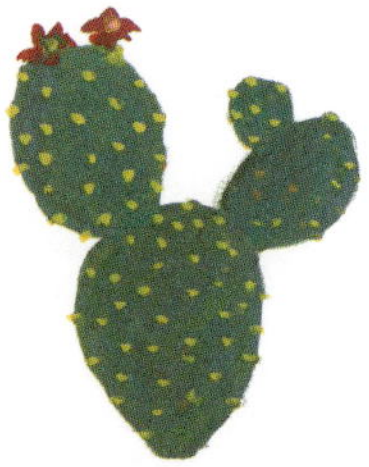

cactus

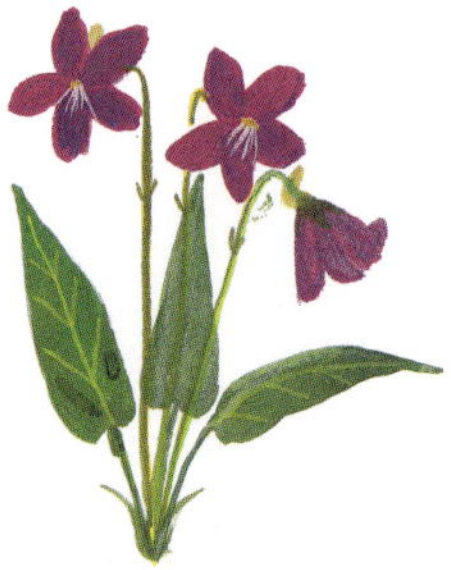

cosmos

violet

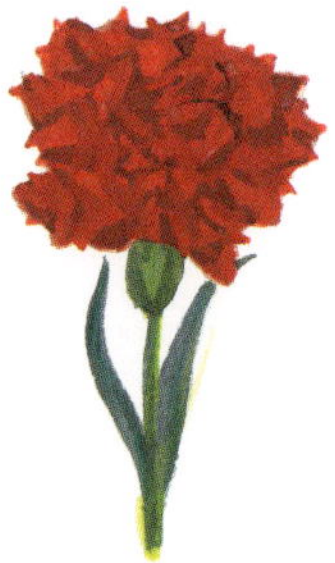

carnation

dandelion

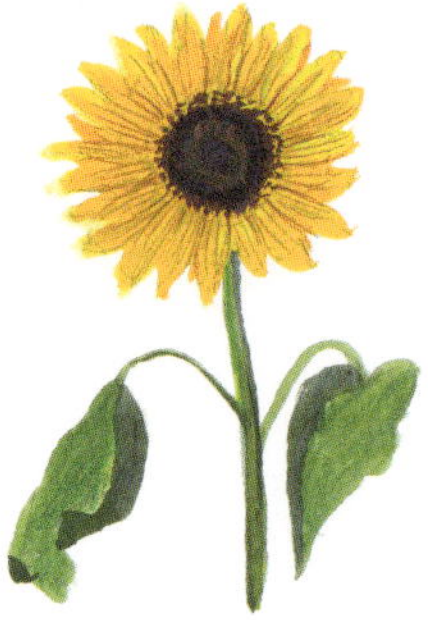

sunflower

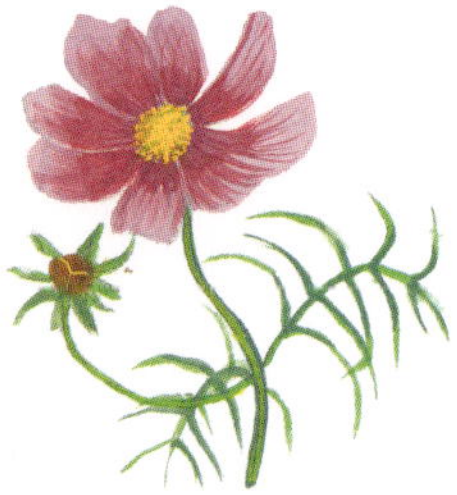

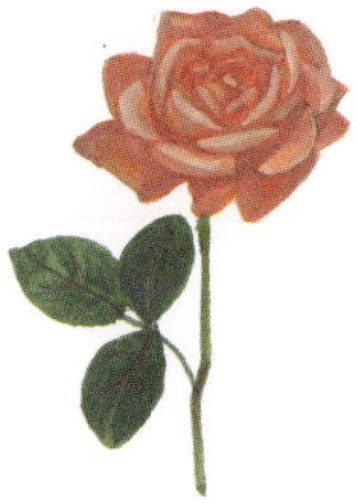

rose

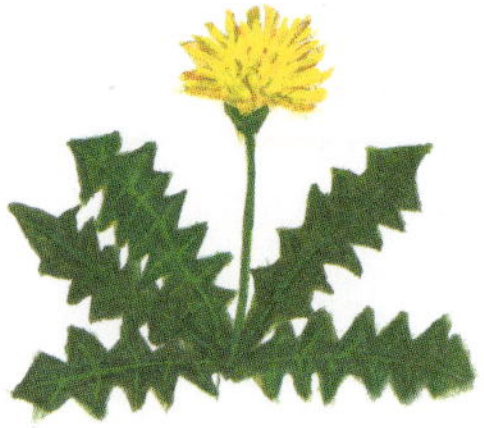

dandelion

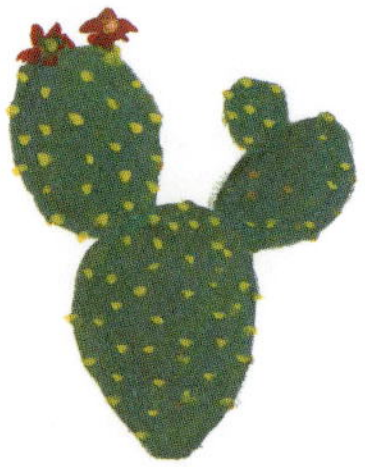

cactus

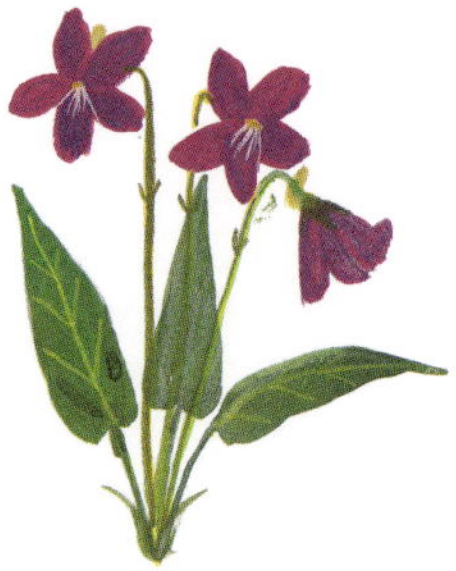

violet

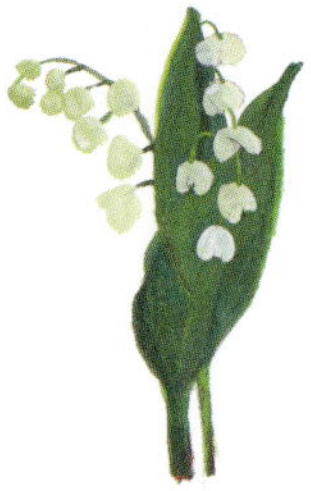

lily of the valley

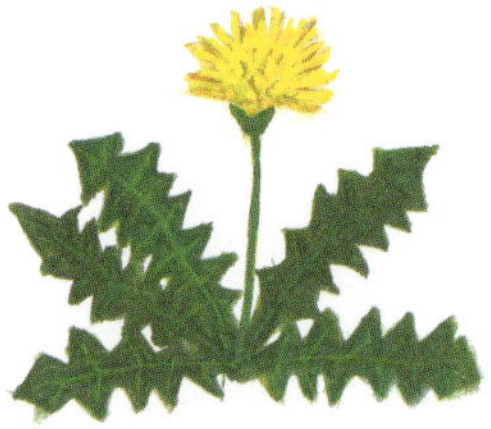

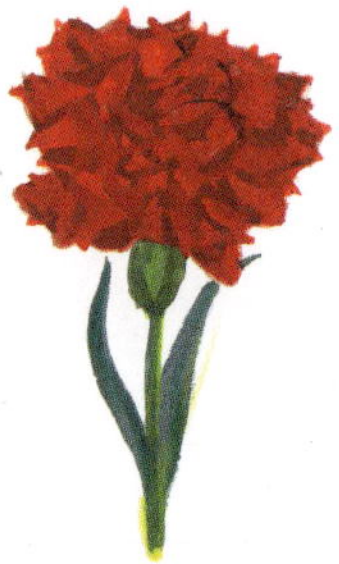

carnation

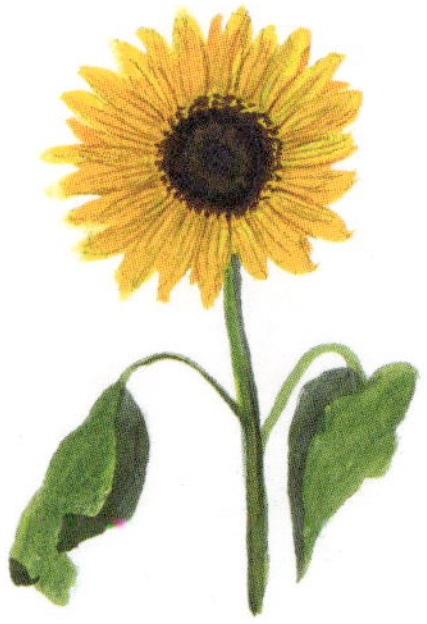

sunflower

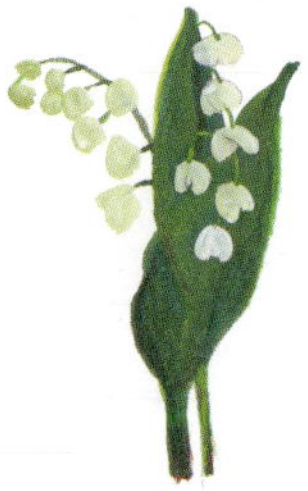

lily of the valley

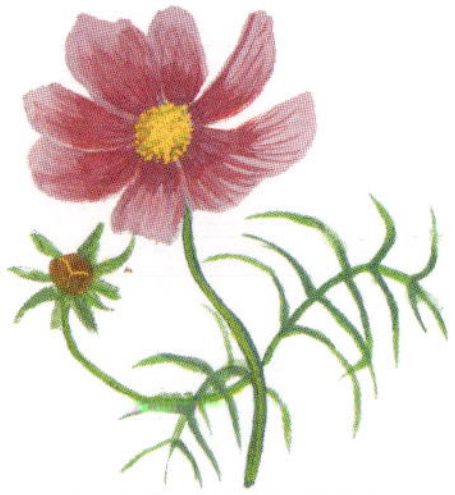

cosmos

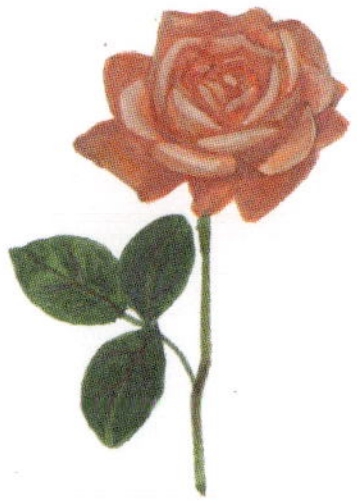

rose

Catch the Bug
(Matching 8)

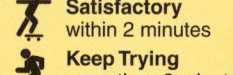

🚀 **Perfect** within 10 seconds	🚌 **Great** within 30 seconds	🚲 **Fair** within 1 minute
✈ **Excellent** within 15 seconds	🚗 **Very good** within 40 seconds	🛹 **Satisfactory** within 2 minutes
🚁 **Super** within 20 seconds	🐎 **Good** within 50 seconds	🏃 **Keep Trying** more than 2 minutes

■ Circle the matching insects.

DATE	NAME	TIME

dragonfly

firefly

cricket

ant

bee

firefly

grasshopper

ant

stag beetle

cicada

cricket

stag beetle

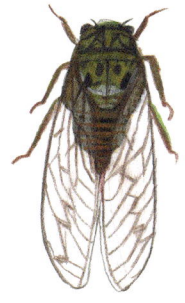

cicada

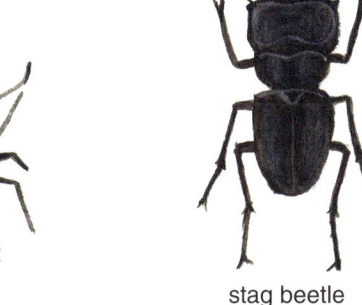

bee

grasshopper

dragonfly

■ Circle the matching birds.

DATE   NAME   TIME

ostrich

peacock

chicken

parrot

chicken

sparrow

parrot

duck

canary

duck

crow

crow

canary

ostrich

sparrow

peacock

■ Circle the matching animals.

DATE   NAME   TIME

elephant

guinea pig

crocodile

panda

tortoise

squirrel

panda

horse

giraffe

crocodile

mole

squirrel

guinea pig

pig

giraffe

pig

elephant

mole

horse

tortoise

DATE   NAME   TIME

■ Circle the matching fish.

ray

catfish

blowfish

carp

eel

carp

sea bream

tuna

loach

blowfish

salmon

loach

ray

anchovy

salmon

eel

tuna

anchovy

catfish

sea bream

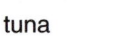

23 At the Farmer's Market (Matching 10)

Perfect within 30 seconds	**Great** within 1 minute	**Fair** within 4 minutes
Excellent within 40 seconds	**Very good** within 2 minutes	**Satisfactory** within 5 minutes
Super within 50 seconds	**Good** within 3 minutes	**Keep Trying** more than 5 minutes

DATE NAME TIME

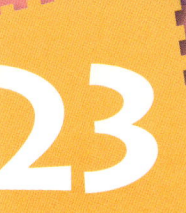

Circle the matching produce.

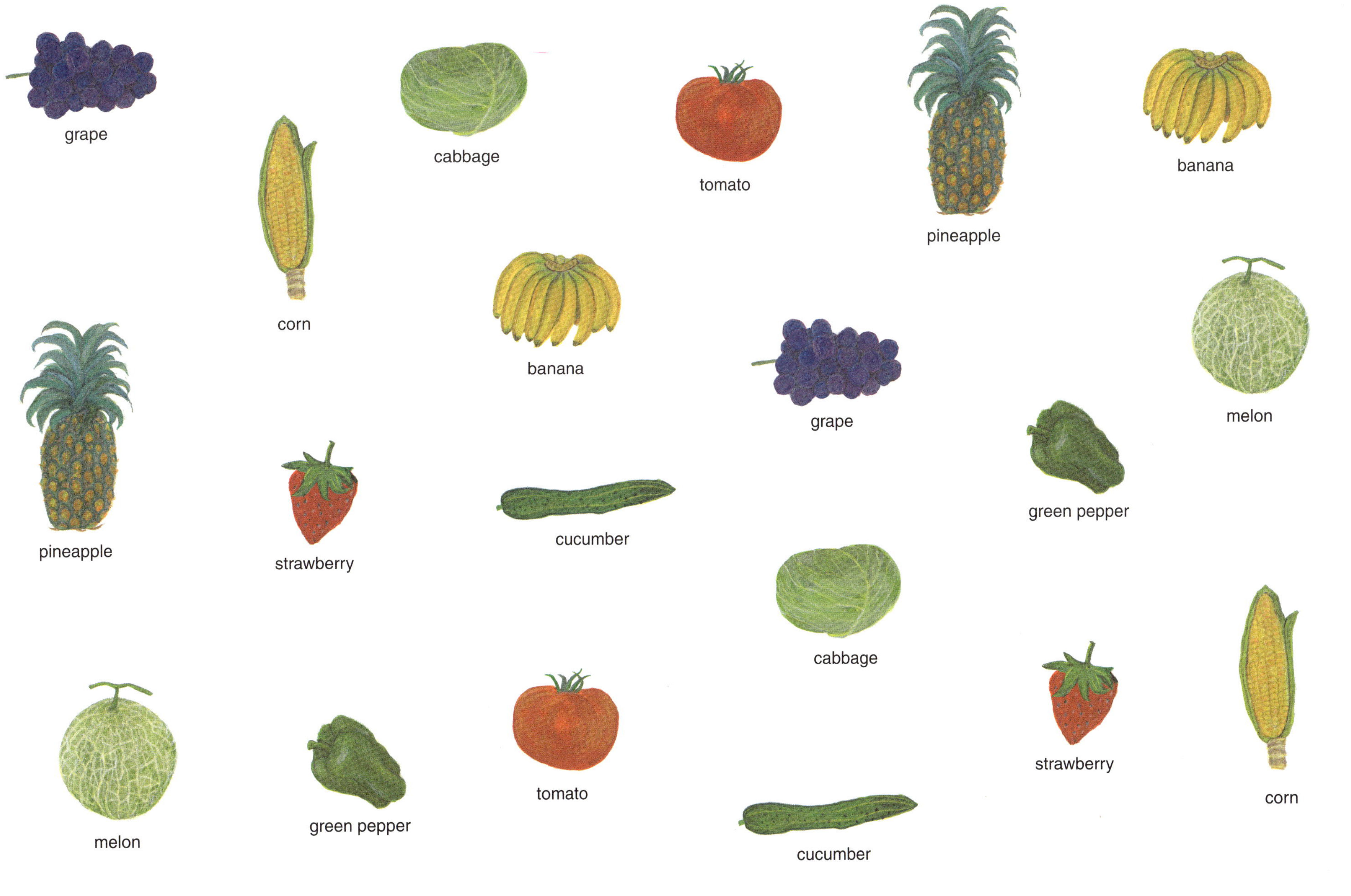

grape
cabbage
tomato
pineapple
banana
corn
banana
grape
melon
pineapple
strawberry
cucumber
green pepper
cabbage
strawberry
corn
melon
green pepper
tomato
cucumber

Circle the matching flowers.

Perfect within 30 seconds	Great within 1 minute	Fair within 4 minutes			
Excellent within 40 seconds	Very good within 2 minutes	Satisfactory within 5 minutes			
Super within 50 seconds	Good within 3 minutes	Keep Trying more than 5 minutes			

DATE   NAME   TIME

violet

lily of the valley

sunflower

hyacinth

cosmos

rose

cosmos

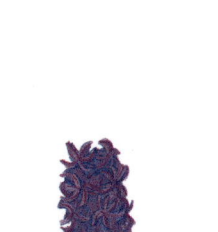

anemone

rose

dandelion

violet

cactus

hyacinth

dandelion

anemone

lily of the valley

sunflower

carnation

cactus

carnation

Catch the Bug

(Matching 10)

■ Circle the matching insects.

DATE   NAME   TIME

stag beetle

cicada

firefly

cricket

scorpion

dragonfly

spider

grasshopper

bee

spider

grasshopper

stag beetle

cricket

ant

firefly

spider

dragonfly

ant

cicada

bee

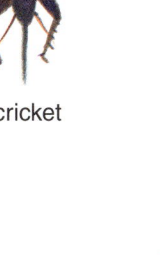
scorpion

Circle the matching birds.

 Perfect within 30 seconds	 Great within 1 minute	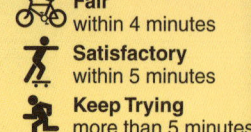 Fair within 4 minutes
Excellent within 40 seconds	Very good within 2 minutes	Satisfactory within 5 minutes
Super within 50 seconds	Good within 3 minutes	Keep Trying more than 5 minutes

DATE   NAME   TIME

owl

peacock

chicken

canary

sparrow

parrot

woodpecker

duck

duck

woodpecker

crow

chicken

ostrich

crow

sparrow

parrot

ostrich

owl

peacock

canary

27 Exploring the Zoo

(Matching 12)

Perfect within 30 seconds
Excellent within 40 seconds
Super within 50 seconds
Great within 1 minute
Very good within 2 minutes
Good within 3 minutes
Fair within 4 minutes
Satisfactory within 5 minutes
Keep Trying more than 5 minutes

DATE NAME TIME

Circle the matching animals.

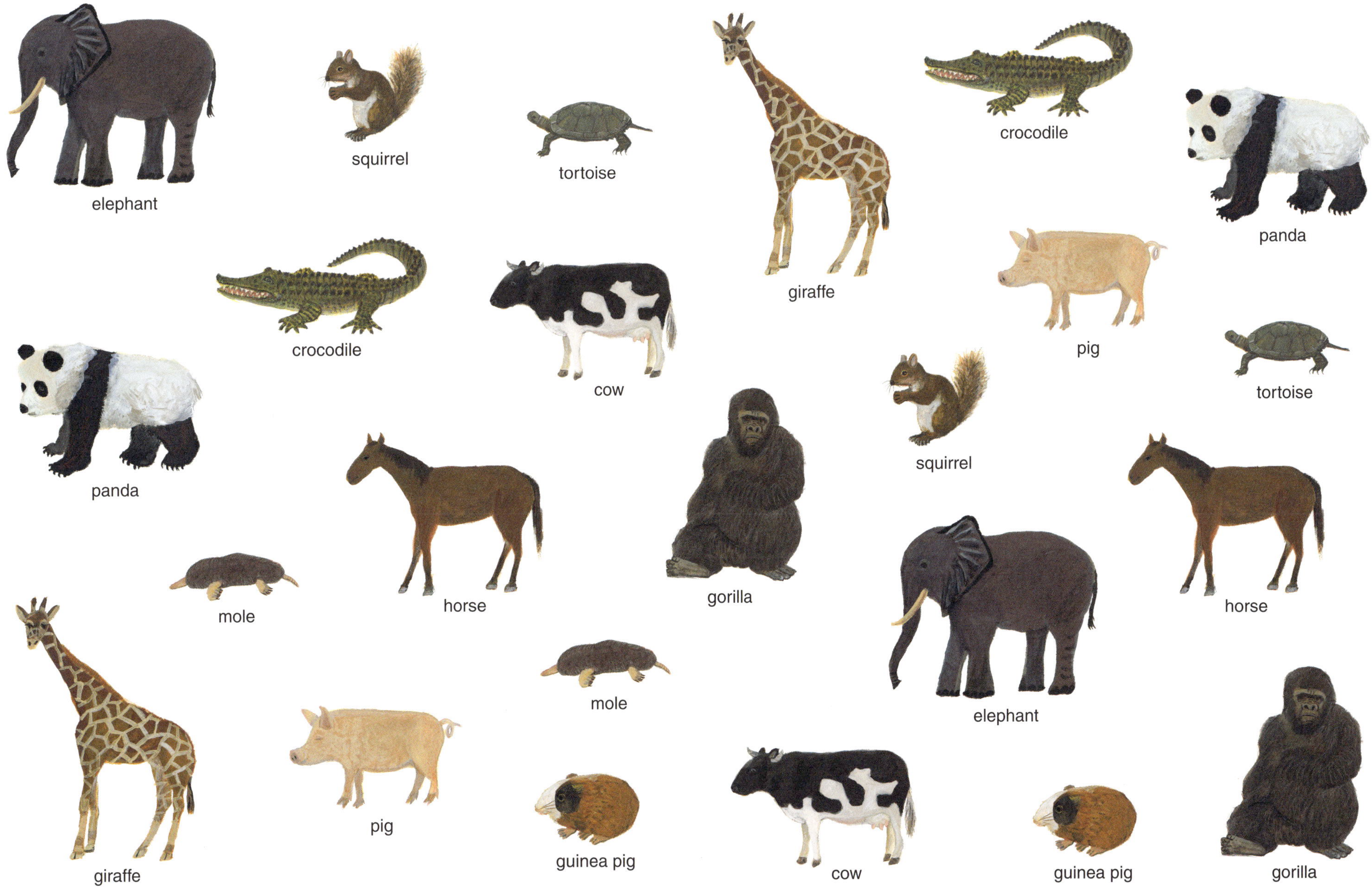
elephant
squirrel
tortoise
giraffe
crocodile
panda
crocodile
cow
pig
tortoise
panda
squirrel
horse
gorilla
horse
mole
mole
elephant
giraffe
pig
guinea pig
cow
guinea pig
gorilla

Dive into the Water

(Matching 12)

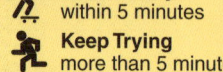
■Circle the matching fish.

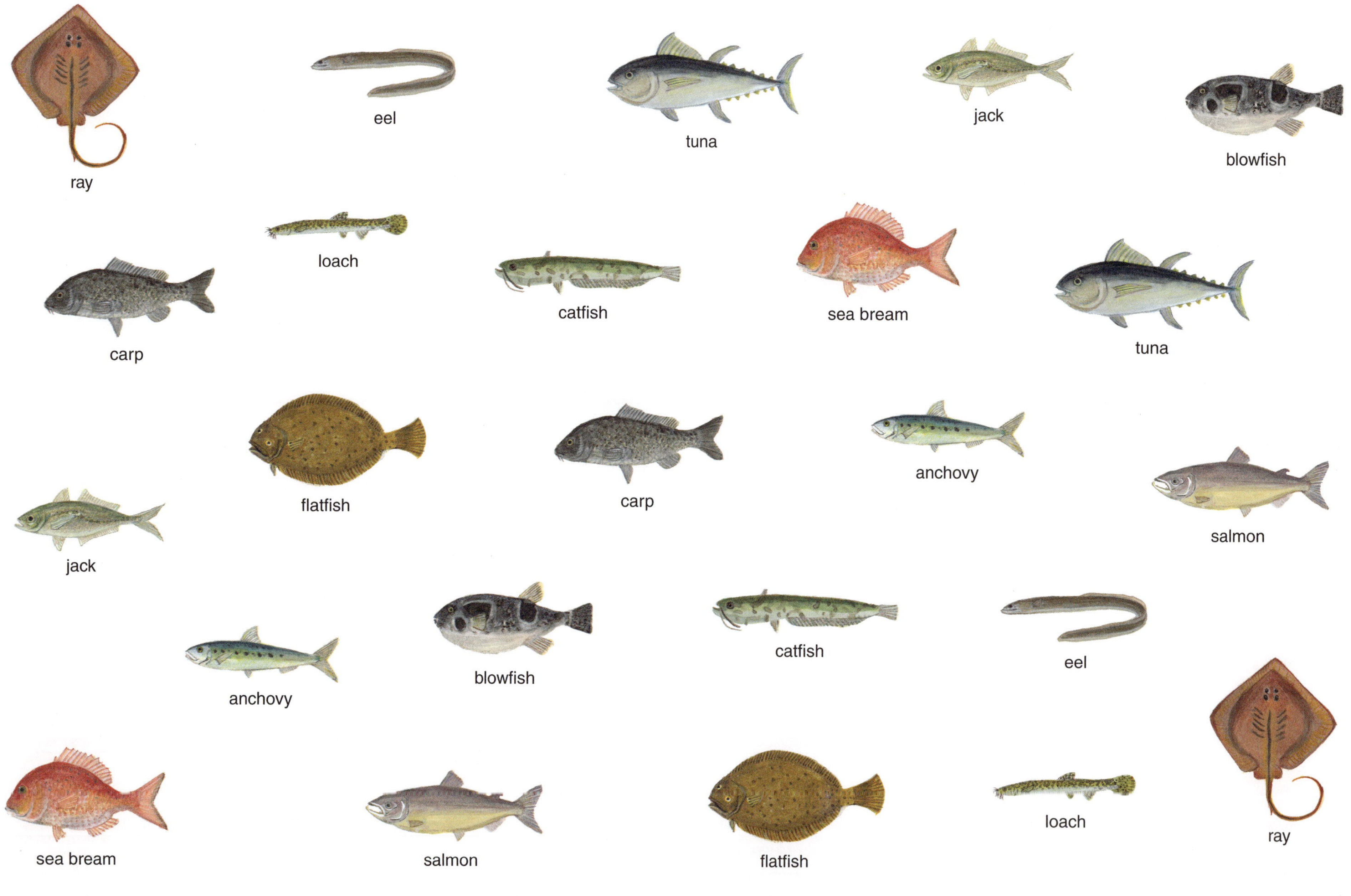

DATE   NAME   TIME

ray

eel

tuna

jack

blowfish

carp

loach

catfish

sea bream

tuna

jack

flatfish

carp

anchovy

salmon

anchovy

blowfish

catfish

eel

sea bream

salmon

flatfish

loach

ray

At the Farmer's Market (Matching 12)

Circle the matching produce.

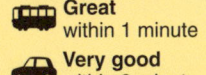

DATE   NAME   TIME

corn

cabbage

cherry

cucumber

pineapple

grape

melon

tomato

banana

strawberry

banana

green pepper

cherry

eggplant

cabbage

green pepper

pineapple

strawberry

melon

corn

tomato

grape

cucumber

eggplant

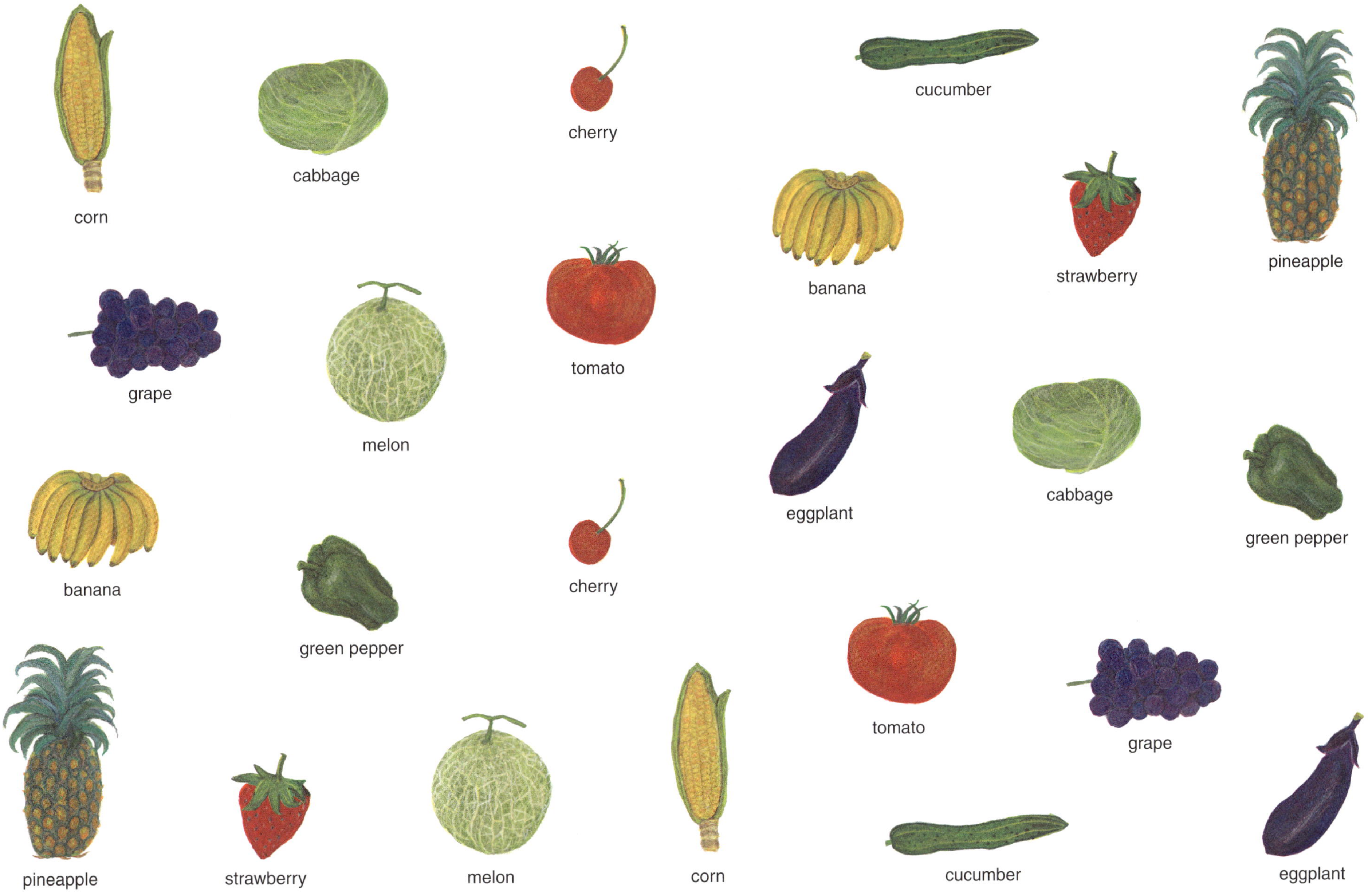

Circle the matching flowers.

DATE　　NAME　　TIME

tulip

carnation

hyacinth

dandelion

dahlia

tulip

anemone

cosmos

rose

sunflower

violet

cactus

hyacinth

lily of the valley

carnation

violet

cosmos

lily of the valley

dahlia

dandelion

cactus

rose

sunflower

anemone

Circle the matching insects.

DATE　　　　NAME　　　　　　　　TIME

long-horned beetle

cricket

butterfly

stag beetle

spider

firefly

bee

grasshopper

cricket

dragonfly

scorpion

spider

firefly

scorpion

ant

cicada

ant

grasshopper

stag beetle

cicada

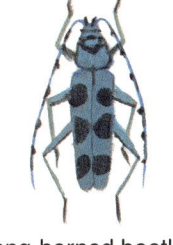

dragonfly

long-horned beetle

bee

butterfly

Birds of a Feather
Stay Together (Matching 12)

🚀 **Perfect** within 30 seconds		🚌 **Great** within 1 minute		🚲 **Fair** within 4 minutes	
✈ **Excellent** within 40 seconds		🚗 **Very good** within 2 minutes		🛴 **Satisfactory** within 5 minutes	
🚁 **Super** within 50 seconds		🐎 **Good** within 3 minutes		🏃 **Keep Trying** more than 5 minutes	

■ Circle the matching birds.

DATE   NAME   TIME

ostrich

woodpecker

owl

wild duck

goose

peacock

crow

wild duck

canary

woodpecker

chicken

duck

canary

sparrow

parrot

sparrow

ostrich

crow

peacock

duck

goose

owl

chicken

parrot

Exploring the Zoo

(Matching 14)

■ Circle the matching animals.

Perfect within 30 seconds	**Great** within 1 minute	**Fair** within 4 minutes
Excellent within 40 seconds	**Very good** within 2 minutes	**Satisfactory** within 5 minutes
Super within 50 seconds	**Good** within 3 minutes	**Keep Trying** more than 5 minutes

DATE   NAME   TIME

elephant

crocodile

rabbit

giraffe

tortoise

mole

panda

squirrel

gorilla

pig

giraffe

squirrel

cow

guinea pig

horse

tortoise

panda

guinea pig

gorilla

crocodile

rabbit

pig

mole

cow

mouse

horse

mouse

elephant

■ Circle the matching fish.

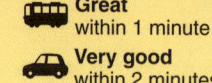
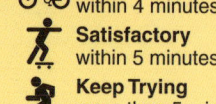
DATE   NAME   TIME

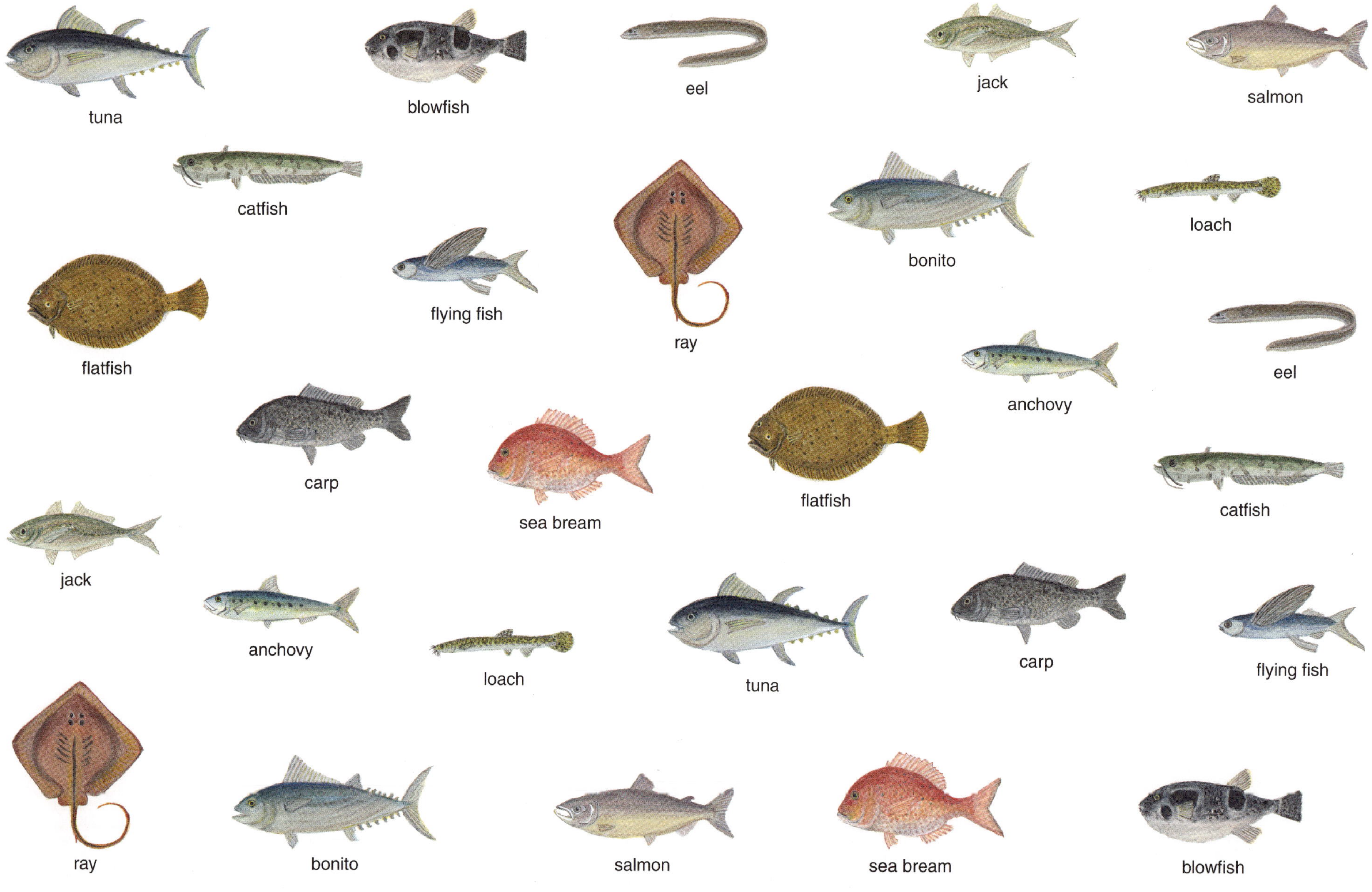

tuna

blowfish

eel

jack

salmon

catfish

flying fish

ray

bonito

loach

flatfish

carp

sea bream

flatfish

anchovy

eel

jack

anchovy

loach

tuna

carp

catfish

ray

bonito

salmon

sea bream

flying fish

blowfish

■ Circle the matching produce.

 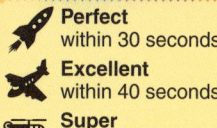
DATE   NAME   TIME

grape

strawberry

tomato

melon

pineapple

eggplant

cucumber

banana

green pepper

cabbage

tomato

strawberry

eggplant

cherry

onion

melon

grape

cabbage

potato

green pepper

cucumber

pineapple

potato

corn

cherry

banana

corn

onion

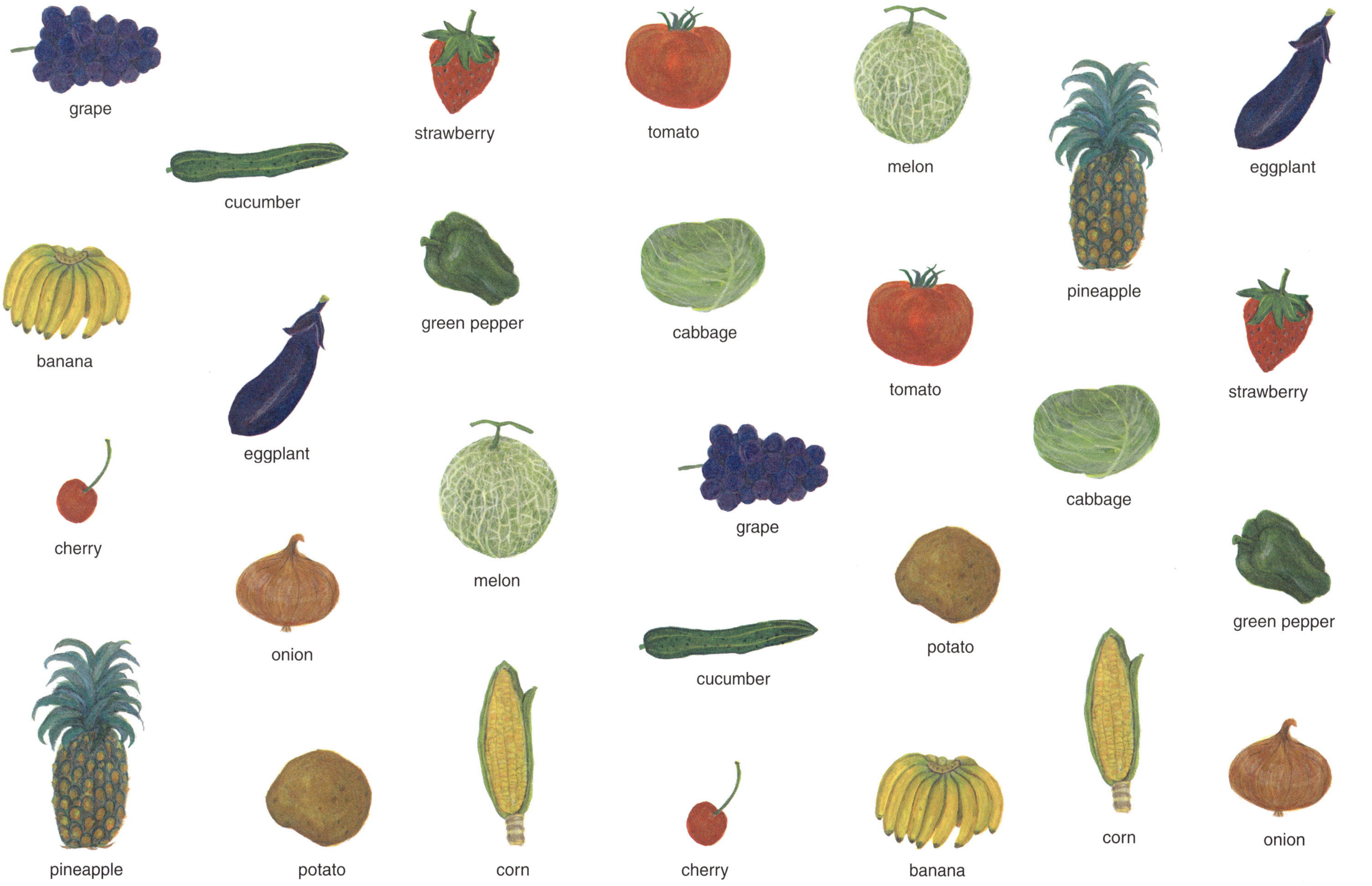

■ Circle the matching flowers.

DATE   NAME   TIME

violet

cactus

lily of the valley

sunflower

tulip

cosmos

hyacinth

dahlia

poppy

anemone

water lily

cactus

carnation

dandelion

hyacinth

tulip

dandelion

rose

lily of the valley

sunflower

rose

 water lily

 cosmos

 violet

 carnation

 poppy

 anemone

 dahlia

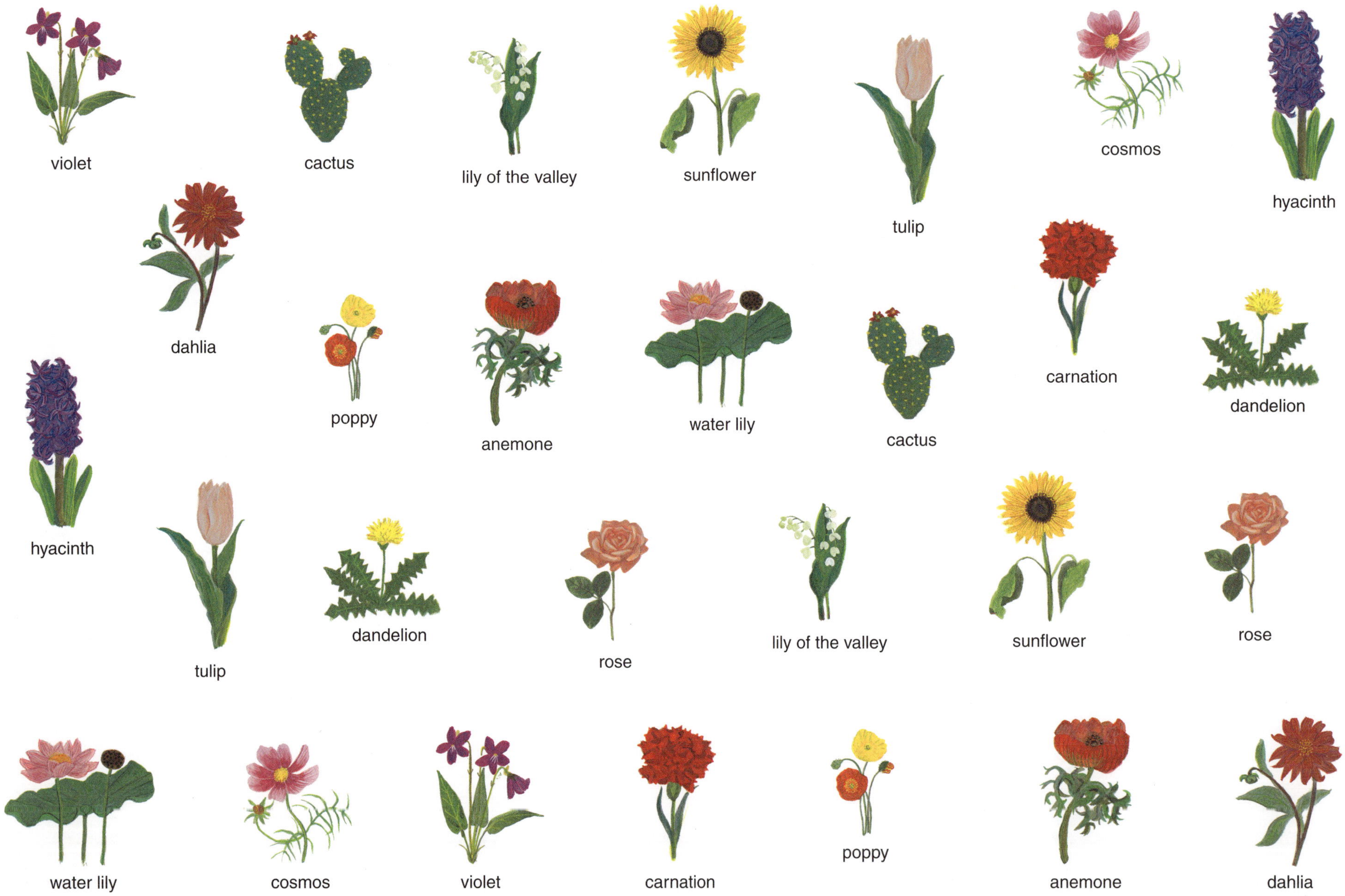

37

Catch the Bug

(Matching 14)

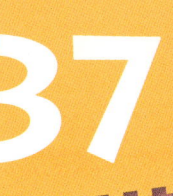

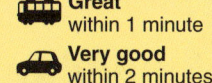

Perfect within 30 seconds
Excellent within 40 seconds
Super within 50 seconds
Great within 1 minute
Very good within 2 minutes
Good within 3 minutes
Fair within 4 minutes
Satisfactory within 5 minutes
Keep Trying more than 5 minutes

Circle the matching insects.

DATE NAME TIME

centipede
scorpion
stag beetle
bee
long-horned beetle
locust
spider
scorpion
butterfly
cricket
ant
firefly
cicada
firefly
dragonfly
grasshopper
spider
locust
bee
stag beetle
grasshopper
long-horned beetle
cicada
dragonfly
centipede
cricket
ant
butterfly

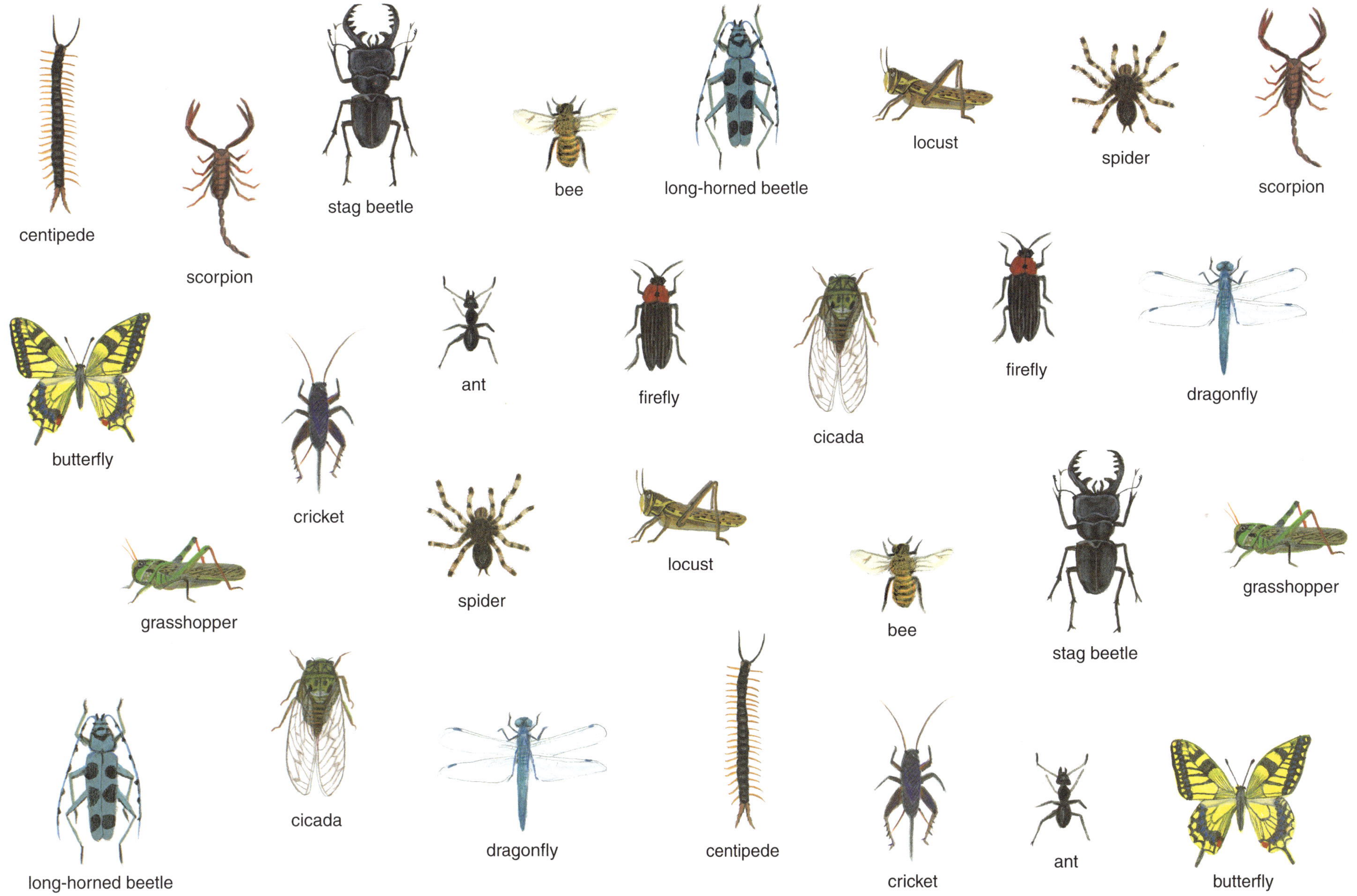

Circle the matching birds.

Perfect within 30 seconds	**Great** within 1 minute	**Fair** within 4 minutes
Excellent within 40 seconds	**Very good** within 2 minutes	**Satisfactory** within 5 minutes
Super within 50 seconds	**Good** within 3 minutes	**Keep Trying** more than 5 minutes

DATE　　　　　　NAME　　　　　　　　TIME

ostrich

wild duck

sparrow

chicken

pigeon

woodpecker

parrot

pelican

peacock

canary

pelican

owl

goose

duck

goose

crow

parrot

sparrow

chicken

crow

canary

pigeon

owl

woodpecker

duck

ostrich

wild duck

peacock

Exploring the Zoo
(Matching 16)

	Perfect within 40 seconds		Great within 2 minutes		Fair within 5 minutes
	Excellent within 50 seconds		Very good within 3 minutes		Satisfactory within 6 minutes
	Super within 1 minute		Good within 4 minutes		Keep Trying more than 6 minutes

■ Circle the matching animals.

DATE   NAME   TIME

elephant   mouse   wild boar   guinea pig   giraffe   rabbit   panda

rabbit   cow   squirrel   pig   gorilla   zebra   wild boar

gorilla   tortoise   horse   tortoise   crocodile   squirrel

panda   mole   zebra   cow   pig   mouse

giraffe   crocodile   guinea pig   elephant   mole   horse

Circle the matching fish.

Perfect within 40 seconds
Excellent within 50 seconds
Super within 1 minute
Great within 2 minutes
Very good within 3 minutes
Good within 4 minutes
Fair within 5 minutes
Satisfactory within 6 minutes
Keep Trying more than 6 minutes

DATE | NAME | TIME

ray

blowfish

catfish

anglerfish

anchovy

jack

bonito

tuna

salmon

goldfish

flatfish

flying fish

sea bream

jack

eel

ray

sea bream

catfish

carp

carp

flying fish

loach

anchovy

bonito

eel

tuna

flatfish

anglerfish

goldfish

blowfish

loach

salmon

DATE   NAME   TIME

■ Circle the matching produce.

pineapple

onion

green pepper

apricot

cucumber

onion

corn

strawberry

potato

corn

strawberry

melon

cucumber

eggplant

asparagus

grape

potato

apricot

grape

banana

grape

asparagus

tomato

green pepper

tomato

cabbage

banana

cherry

cabbage

pineapple

melon

cherry

eggplant

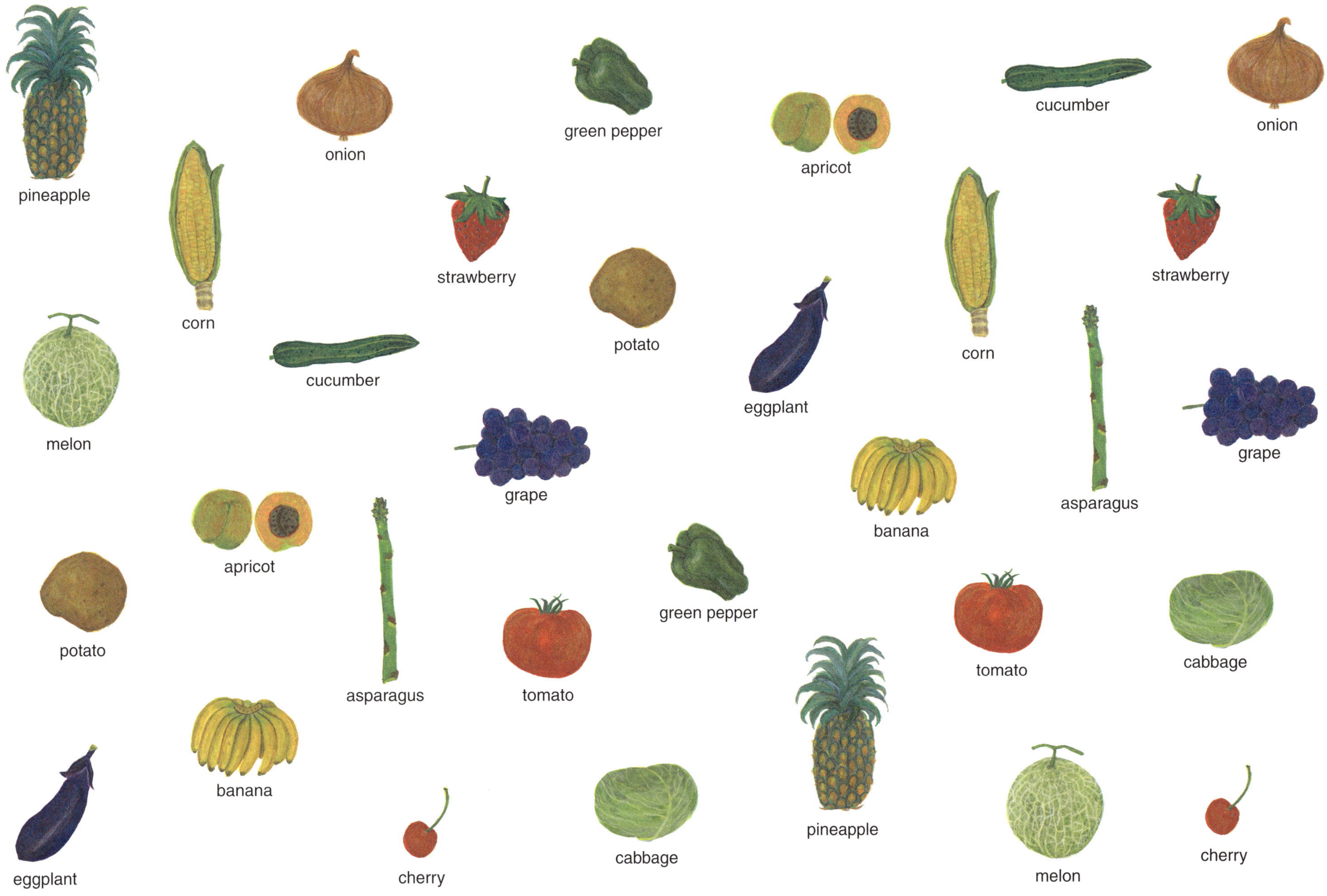

Picking Flowers

(Matching 16)

	Perfect		Great		Fair
	within 40 seconds		within 2 minutes		within 5 minutes
	Excellent		Very good		Satisfactory
	within 50 seconds		within 3 minutes		within 6 minutes
	Super		Good		Keep Trying
	within 1 minute		within 4 minutes		more than 6 minutes

■ Circle the matching flowers.

DATE	NAME	TIME

dandelion

rose

cosmos

hyacinth

violet

cactus

sunflower

lily of the valley

marguerite

water lily

carnation

clover

rose

carnation

dandelion

tulip

poppy

cactus

sunflower

anemone

marguerite

water lily

dahlia

clover

violet

dahlia

tulip

poppy

cosmos

anemone

hyacinth

lily of the valley

Catch the Bug

(Matching 16)

Circle the matching insects.

🚀 **Perfect** within 40 seconds	🚌 **Great** within 2 minutes	🚲 **Fair** within 5 minutes
✈️ **Excellent** within 50 seconds	🚗 **Very good** within 3 minutes	🛹 **Satisfactory** within 6 minutes
🚁 **Super** within 1 minute	🐴 **Good** within 4 minutes	🏃 **Keep Trying** more than 6 minutes

DATE   NAME   TIME

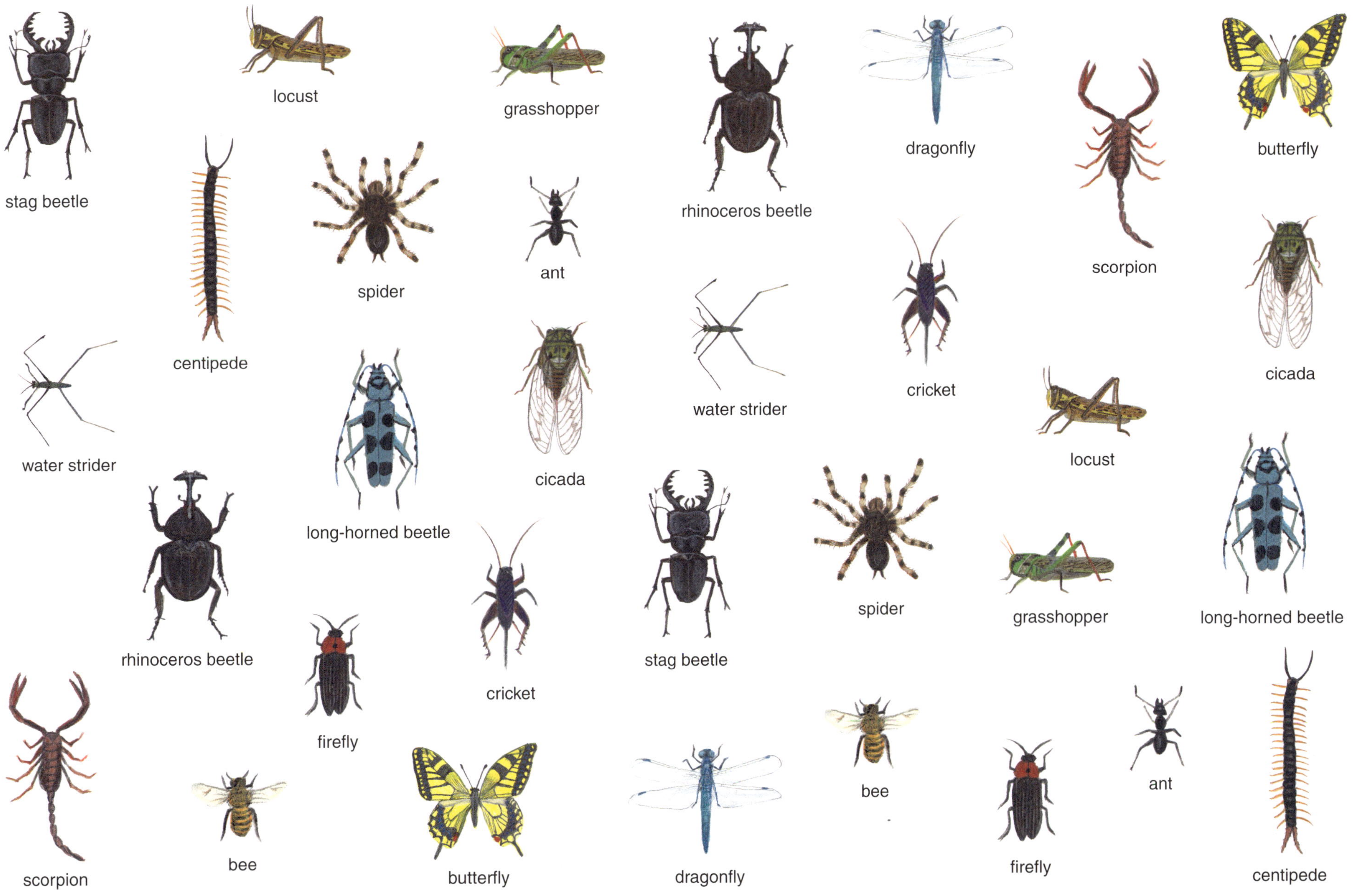

locust

grasshopper

dragonfly

butterfly

stag beetle

rhinoceros beetle

scorpion

centipede

spider

ant

scorpion

cicada

water strider

cricket

water strider

cicada

locust

long-horned beetle

rhinoceros beetle

long-horned beetle

firefly

cricket

stag beetle

spider

grasshopper

scorpion

bee

butterfly

dragonfly

bee

firefly

ant

centipede

44

Birds of a Feather Stay Together (Matching 16)

■ Circle the matching birds.

|---|---|---|
Perfect within 40 seconds	**Great** within 2 minutes	**Fair** within 5 minutes
Excellent within 50 seconds	**Very good** within 3 minutes	**Satisfactory** within 6 minutes
Super within 1 minute	**Good** within 4 minutes	**Keep Trying** more than 6 minutes

DATE　　　NAME　　　TIME

Exploring the Zoo

(Matching 18)

■ Circle the matching animals.

	Perfect within 40 seconds	Great within 2 minutes	Fair within 5 minutes
	Excellent within 50 seconds	Very good within 3 minutes	Satisfactory within 6 minutes
	Super within 1 minute	Good within 4 minutes	Keep Trying more than 6 minutes

DATE   NAME   TIME

panda

rhinoceros

horse

cow

pig

gorilla

mole

zebra

guinea pig

elephant

fox

panda

tortoise

fox

mouse

giraffe

mole

crocodile

wild boar

mouse

gorilla

cow

rabbit

wild boar

zebra

squirrel

pig

tortoise

crocodile

wild boar

zebra

guinea pig

giraffe

elephant

squirrel

rhinoceros

rabbit

horse

Dive into the Water
(Matching 18)

Circle the matching fish.

 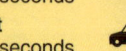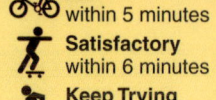
DATE   NAME   TIME

anglerfish

carp

salmon

flatfish

flying fish

sea horse

goldfish

angelfish

jack

anchovy

loach

bonito

ray

jack

blowfish

sea horse

sea bream

angelfish

goldfish

flatfish

catfish

eel

anglerfish

loach

bonito

ray

tuna

carp

anchovy

salmon

blowfish

flying fish

eel

catfish

tuna

sea bream

■ Circle the matching produce.

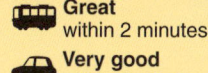
DATE   NAME   TIME

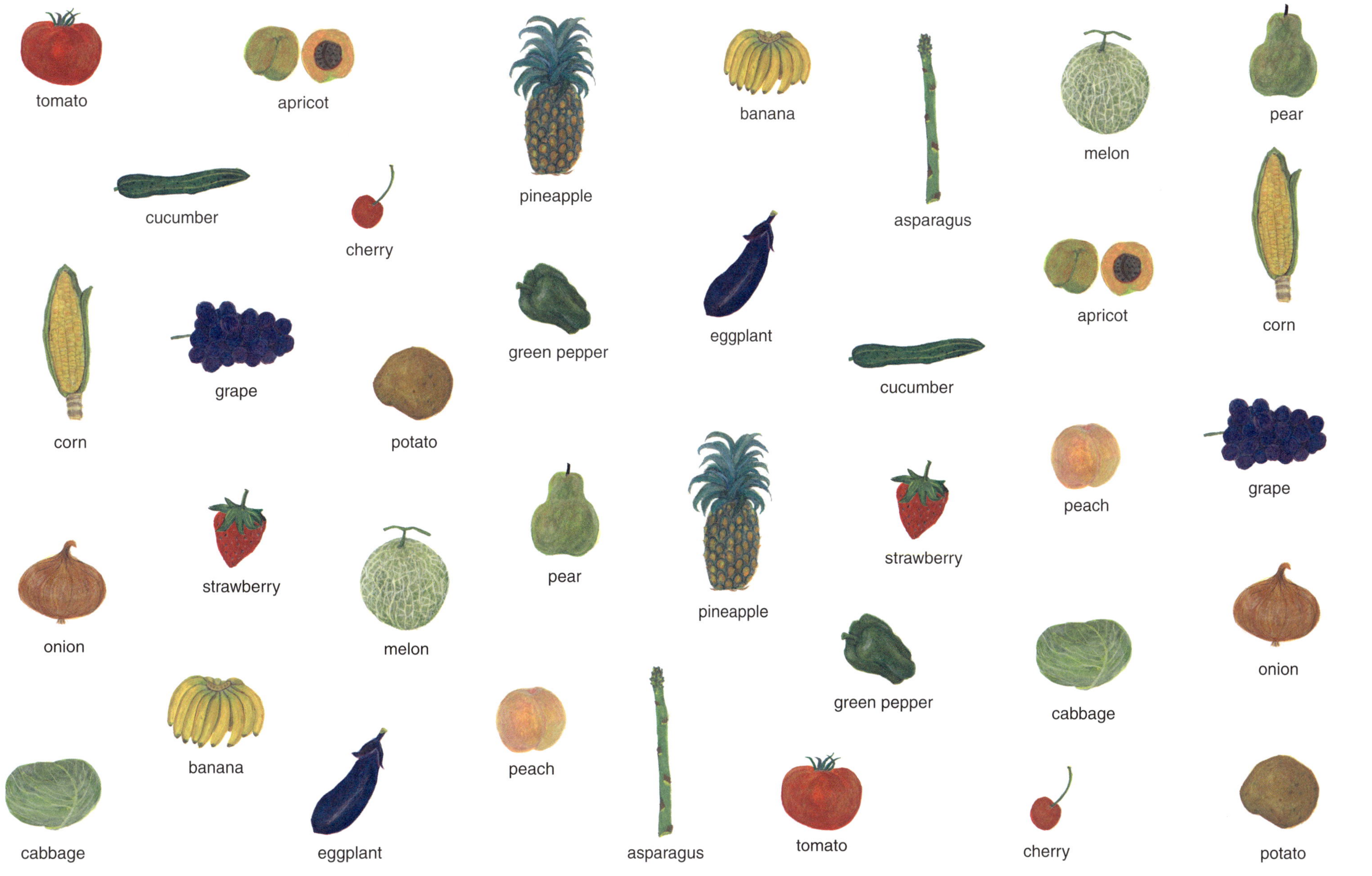

tomato

apricot

pineapple

banana

asparagus

melon

pear

cucumber

cherry

green pepper

eggplant

apricot

corn

corn

grape

potato

cucumber

grape

onion

strawberry

melon

pear

pineapple

strawberry

peach

onion

banana

eggplant

peach

asparagus

green pepper

cabbage

cabbage

tomato

cherry

potato

48 Picking Flowers

(Matching 18)

Circle the matching flowers.

	Perfect within 40 seconds		Great within 2 minutes		Fair within 5 minutes
Excellent within 50 seconds		Very good within 3 minutes		Satisfactory within 6 minutes
Super within 1 minute		Good within 4 minutes		Keep Trying more than 6 minutes

DATE   NAME   TIME

rose

salvia

lily of the valley

cactus

water lily

dahlia

sunflower

carnation

chrysanthemum

tulip

marguerite

hyacinth

clover

anemone

rose

violet

lily of the valley

carnation

dahlia

cosmos

tulip

water lily

cosmos

hyacinth

violet

clover

dandelion

poppy

cactus

chrysanthemum

marguerite

poppy

salvia

sunflower

dandelion

anemone

Catch the Bug
(Matching 18)

Circle the matching insects.

DATE   NAME   TIME

bee

butterfly

scorpion

rhinoceros beetle

mole cricket

centipede

spider

dragonfly

katydid

firefly

stag beetle

cicada

grasshopper

water strider

firefly

ant

long-horned beetle

long-horned beetle

locust

dragonfly

cricket

grasshopper

stag beetle

butterfly

ant

cricket

cicada

locust

bee

centipede

spider

katydid

mole cricket

rhinoceros beetle

scorpion

water strider

50
Birds of a Feather Stay Together (Matching 18)

	Perfect within 40 seconds		Great within 2 minutes		Fair within 5 minutes
	Excellent within 50 seconds		Very good within 3 minutes		Satisfactory within 6 minutes
	Super within 1 minute		Good within 4 minutes		Keep Trying more than 6 minutes

■ Circle the matching birds.

DATE   NAME   TIME

eagle · goose · canary · chicken · sparrow · ostrich · owl

wild duck · hawk · wild duck · kingfisher

turkey · owl · pigeon · chicken · woodpecker · peacock

parrot · duck · canary

hawk · sparrow · goose

pelican · peacock · pelican · crow

pigeon · duck · turkey

ostrich · woodpecker · crow · eagle · kingfisher · parrot

51 Exploring the Zoo

(Matching 20)

■ Circle the matching animals.

🚀 **Perfect** within 40 seconds	🚌 **Great** within 2 minutes	🚲 **Fair** within 5 minutes
✈ **Excellent** within 50 seconds	🚗 **Very good** within 3 minutes	🛹 **Satisfactory** within 6 minutes
🚁 **Super** within 1 minute	🐎 **Good** within 4 minutes	🏃 **Keep Trying** more than 6 minutes

DATE   NAME   TIME

giraffe

wild boar

mole

tiger

tortoise

rhinoceros

gorilla

crocodile

tiger

pig

horse

squirrel

zebra

cow

fox

cow

panda

fox

hippopotamus

cow

crocodile

tiger

mouse

pig

elephant

mole

rabbit

squirrel

horse

rhinoceros

gorilla

hippopotamus

guinea pig

tortoise

elephant

panda

rabbit

guinea pig

zebra

wild boar

mouse

giraffe

52 Dive into the Water

(Matching 20)

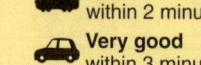

Perfect within 40 seconds	**Great** within 2 minutes
Excellent within 50 seconds	**Very good** within 3 minutes
Super within 1 minute	**Good** within 4 minutes
Fair within 5 minutes	**Satisfactory** within 6 minutes
Keep Trying more than 6 minutes	

Circle the matching fish.

DATE NAME TIME

salmon
bonito
flying fish
sea bream
catfish
carp
salmon
shark
angelfish
tuna
flatfish
eel
sunfish
jack
ray
flatfish
bonito
carp
loach
tuna
sea horse
anchovy
shark
goldfish
blowfish
loach
anglerfish
sea horse
eel
jack
anglerfish
blowfish
goldfish
sunfish
catfish
sea bream
angelfish
flying fish
anchovy
ray

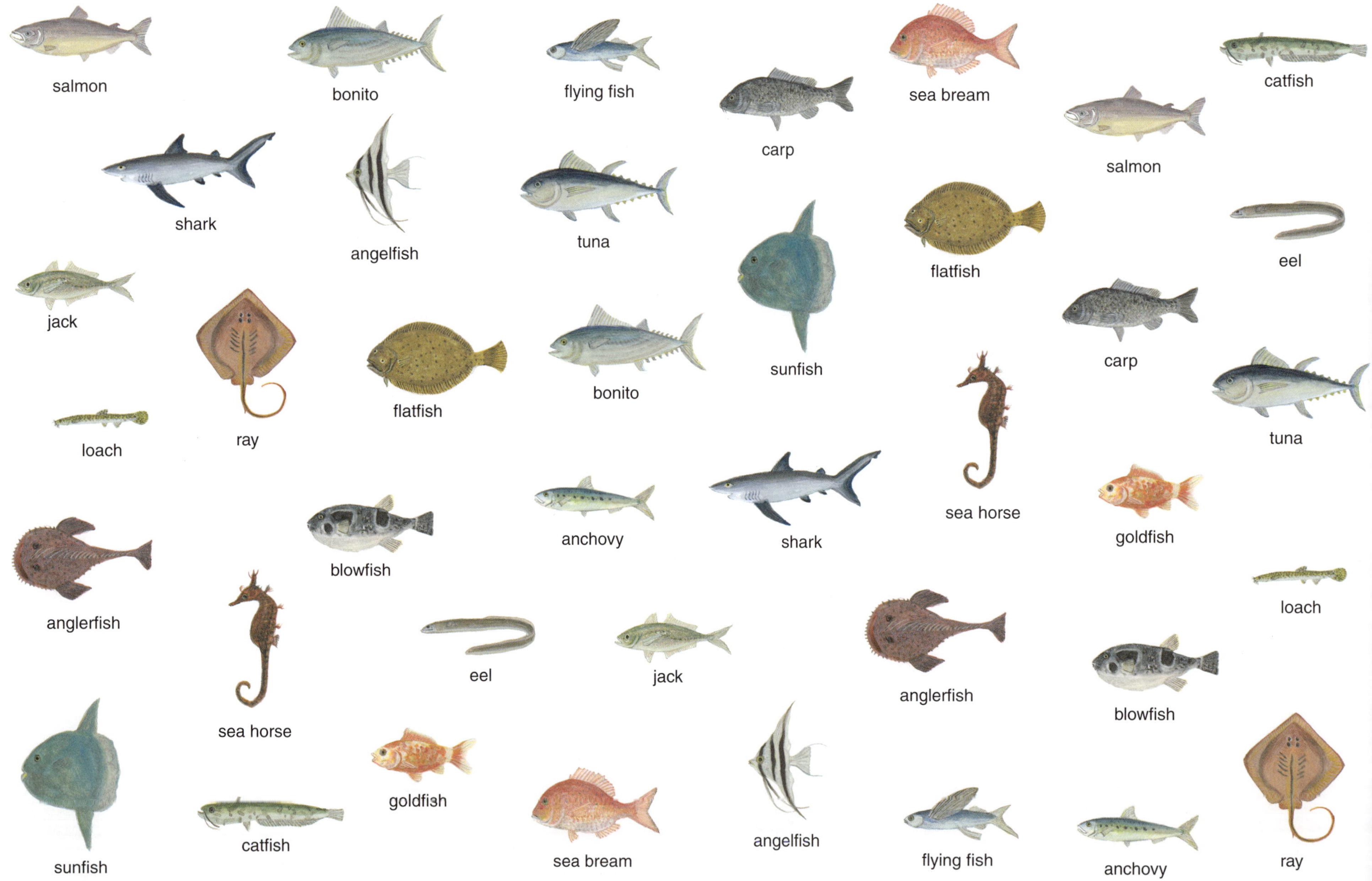

53 At the Farmer's Market (Matching 20)

Perfect within 40 seconds
Excellent within 50 seconds
Super within 1 minute
Great within 2 minutes
Very good within 3 minutes
Good within 4 minutes
Fair within 5 minutes
Satisfactory within 6 minutes
Keep Trying more than 6 minutes

DATE NAME TIME

Circle the matching produce.

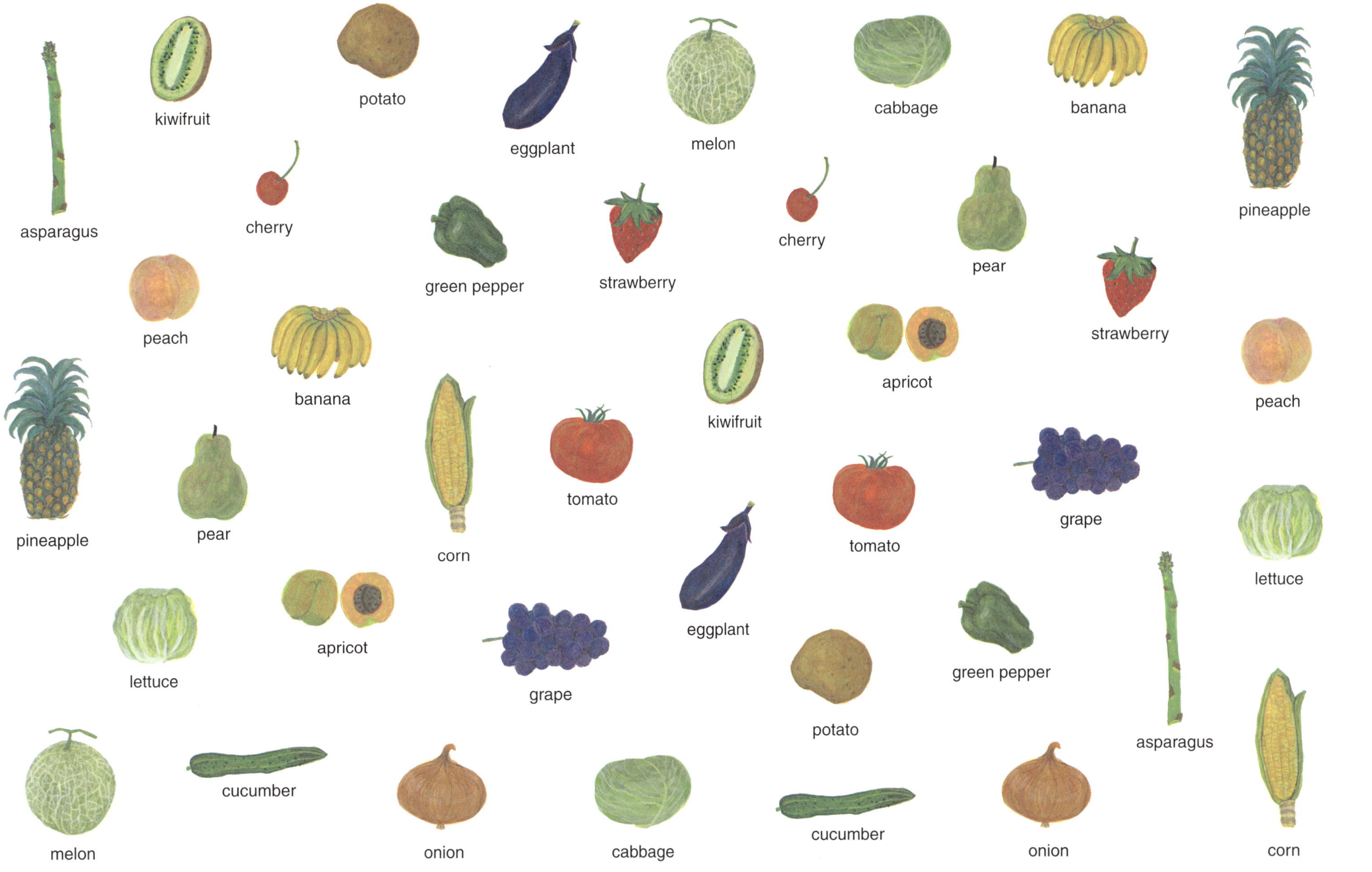

asparagus
kiwifruit
potato
eggplant
melon
cabbage
banana
pineapple
cherry
green pepper
strawberry
cherry
pear
strawberry
peach
banana
kiwifruit
apricot
peach
pineapple
pear
corn
tomato
tomato
grape
lettuce
lettuce
apricot
grape
eggplant
potato
green pepper
asparagus
melon
cucumber
onion
cabbage
cucumber
onion
corn

Picking Flowers

(Matching 20)

■ Circle the matching flowers.

DATE   NAME   TIME

rose

sunflower

salvia

marguerite

carnation

water lily

cactus

poppy

violet

gerbera

hyacinth

cherry blossoms

cosmos

dandelion

rose

chrysanthemum

violet

anemone

lily of the valley

salvia

tulip

marguerite

dahlia

chrysanthemum

clover

carnation

poppy

dandelion

tulip

dahlia

cosmos

lily of the valley

clover

water lily

gerbera

cactus

hyacinth

cherry blossoms

anemone

sunflower

Catch the Bug

(Matching 20)

■ Circle the matching insects.

🚀 **Perfect** within 40 seconds	🚌 **Great** within 2 minutes	🚲 **Fair** within 5 minutes
✈️ **Excellent** within 50 seconds	🚗 **Very good** within 3 minutes	🛹 **Satisfactory** within 6 minutes
🚁 **Super** within 1 minute	🐴 **Good** within 4 minutes	🧗 **Keep Trying** more than 6 minutes

DATE   NAME   TIME

ant

long-horned beetle

dragonfly

rhinoceros beetle

cockroach

locust

long-horned beetle

butterfly

scorpion

mole cricket

water strider

grasshopper

water strider

firefly

bee

jewel beetle

spider

locust

bee

grasshopper

spider

centipede

katydid

spider

cricket

scorpion

ant

mole cricket

stag beetle

cricket

cockroach

dragonfly

cicada

stag beetle

rhinoceros beetle

firefly

cicada

jewel beetle

butterfly

cicada

centipede

katydid

Circle the matching birds.

🚀	**Perfect** within 40 seconds	🚌	**Great** within 2 minutes	🚲	**Fair** within 5 minutes
✈️	**Excellent** within 50 seconds	🚗	**Very good** within 3 minutes	🛹	**Satisfactory** within 6 minutes
🚁	**Super** within 1 minute	🐎	**Good** within 4 minutes	🚶	**Keep Trying** more than 6 minutes

DATE   NAME   TIME

eagle
chicken
canary
sea gull
woodpecker
hawk
chicken
parrot
owl
duck
crow
turkey
wild duck
sparrow
pelican
wild duck
sparrow
magpie
goose
owl
kingfisher
eagle
woodpecker
duck
canary
ostrich
pelican
hawk
sea gull
kingfisher
pigeon
crow
peacock
peacock
pigeon
parrot
turkey
magpie
goose
ostrich

All Objects (Matching 20)

 **Perfect** within 40 seconds
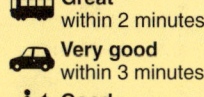 **Great** within 2 minutes
Fair within 5 minutes

Excellent within 50 seconds
Very good within 3 minutes
Satisfactory within 6 minutes

Super within 1 minute
Good within 4 minutes
Keep Trying more than 6 minutes

Circle the matching objects.

DATE   NAME   TIME

giraffe

grasshopper

sunflower

tomato

chicken

ray

panda

bee

duck

tuna

eel

rose

squirrel

tuna

ant

strawberry

elephant

green pepper

duck

strawberry

ant

chicken

bee

lily of the valley

tomato

squirrel

giraffe

salmon

lily of the valley

rose

parrot

salmon

parrot

grasshopper

green pepper

ray

panda

sunflower

giraffe

eel

elephant

58

All Objects (Matching 20)

■ Circle the matching objects.

Perfect	Great	Fair
within 40 seconds	within 2 minutes	within 5 minutes
Excellent	Very good	Satisfactory
within 50 seconds	within 3 minutes	within 6 minutes
Super	Good	Keep Trying
within 1 minute	within 4 minutes	more than 6 minutes

DATE   NAME   TIME

corn

crow

crocodile

guinea pig

anchovy

loach

peacock

cucumber

blowfish

cricket

crocodile

tortoise

cactus

carnation

stag beetle

grape

cicada

mole

carnation

guinea pig

mole

cicada

canary

cactus

canary

cucumber

stag beetle

cricket

canary

blowfish

tortoise

anchovy

carp

peacock

carp

violet

loach

corn

violet

crow

grape

Circle the matching objects.

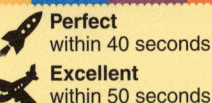 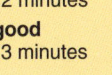

gorilla

flatfish

jack

woodpecker

firefly

cosmos

dragonfly

banana

melon

dandelion

cow

sparrow

banana

ostrich

spider

firefly

cabbage

anemone

cosmos

pig

gorilla

flatfish

sea bream

anemone

cabbage

ostrich

spider

dandelion

anemone

horse

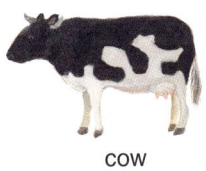
cow

catfish

melon

jack

sea bream

horse

dragonfly

sparrow

woodpecker

catfish

pig

■ Circle the matching objects.

DATE   NAME   TIME

wild boar

eggplant

butterfly

tulip

goldfish

scorpion

eggplant

zebra

long-horned beetle

pineapple

dahlia

owl

goose

wild duck

dahlia

bonito

goose

long-horned beetle

mouse

anglerfish

cherry

tulip

wild boar

rabbit

hyacinth

owl

cherry

flying fish

hyacinth

bonito

flying fish

wild duck

mouse

goldfish

pineapple

rabbit

zebra

scorpion

butterfly

anglerfish

All Objects (Matching 20)

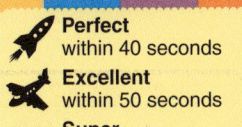
■ Circle the matching objects.

DATE   NAME   TIME

hippopotamus

onion

pelican

apricot

locust

fox

apricot

rhinoceros

sunfish

poppy

centipede

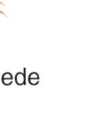
tiger

water lily

potato

clover

onion

pigeon

rhinoceros

kingfisher

potato

locust

sea horse

kingfisher

poppy

sea horse

centipede

fox

angelfish

water lily

pigeon

sunfish

shark

pelican

shark

clover

water strider

tiger

water strider

angelfish

hippopotamus

62 All Objects (Matching 20)

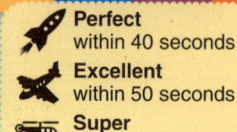

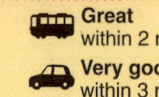

Perfect within 40 seconds
Excellent within 50 seconds
Super within 1 minute
Great within 2 minutes
Very good within 3 minutes
Good within 4 minutes
Fair within 5 minutes
Satisfactory within 6 minutes
Keep Trying more than 6 minutes

Circle the matching objects.

DATE NAME TIME

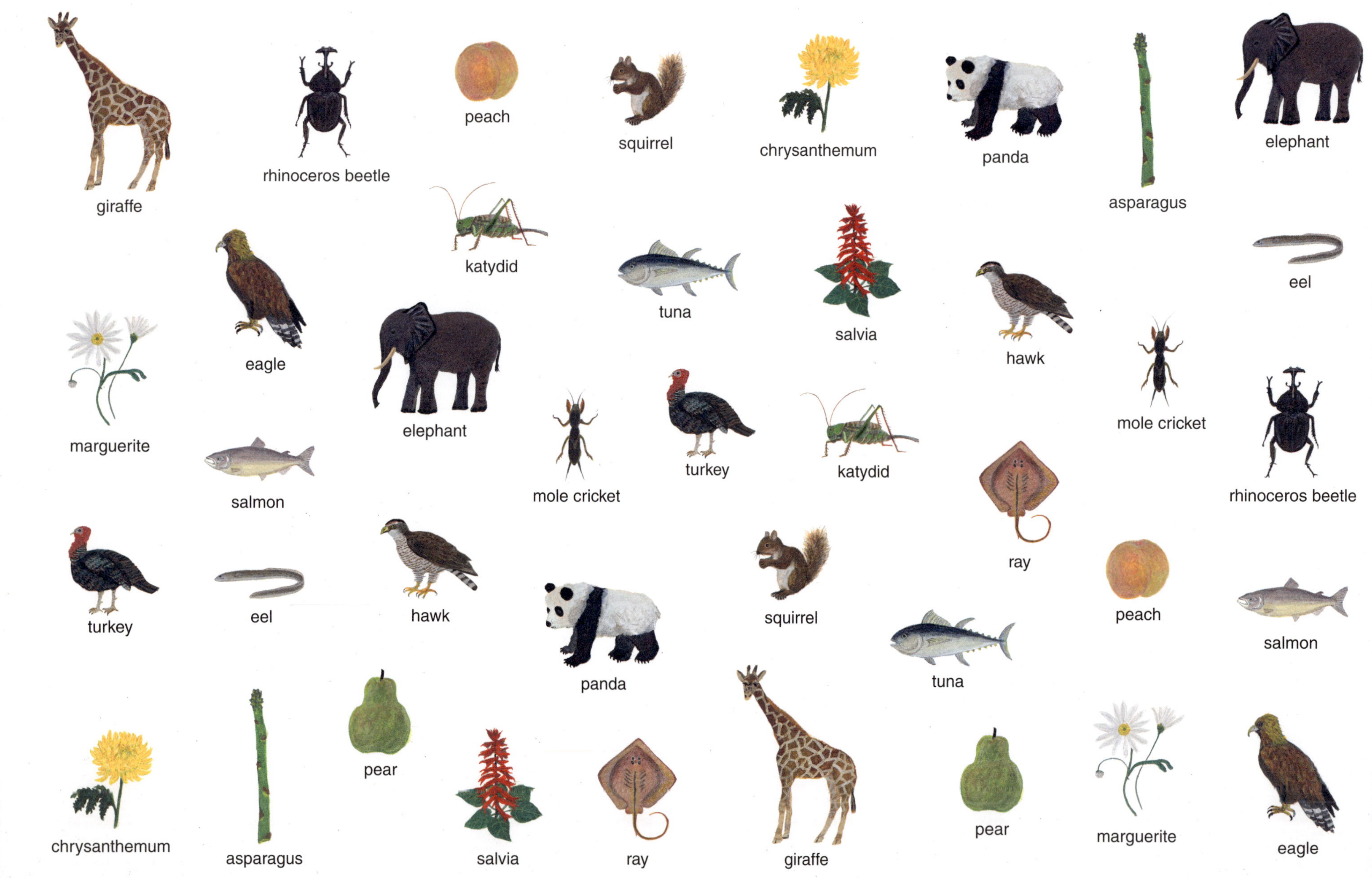

giraffe
rhinoceros beetle
peach
squirrel
chrysanthemum
panda
asparagus
elephant
katydid
eagle
tuna
salvia
hawk
eel
marguerite
elephant
mole cricket
turkey
katydid
mole cricket
rhinoceros beetle
salmon
ray
turkey
eel
hawk
squirrel
panda
peach
salmon
tuna
pear
chrysanthemum
asparagus
salvia
ray
giraffe
pear
marguerite
eagle